The Thing in the Cupboard

Chris Powling ✖ Jonatronix

OXFORD
UNIVERSITY PRESS

Chapter 1 - Lost property

Tiger was in a sulk.

"I didn't kick the ball," he grumbled. "I just dropped it."

"Three times?" laughed Cat. "No wonder Miss Jones took the ball off you."

"I am captain of the football team. That means I've got to practise."

"Well, you'll have to practise being nice to Miss Jones if you want your ball back," said Max.

Store Cupboard

Tiger watched Miss Jones open the door to the store cupboard and put the ball inside. She pushed the door to. Tiger sulked even more.

Chapter 2 - Spiders

Miss Jones lifted a finger to her lips.

"Shush!" she said. "For today's drama lesson I want you all to be spiders."

Tiger sat very still. His face was as white as the lines on a football pitch. He was scared stiff of spiders.

Miss Jones crept round the hall in a spidery way. "I want you all to spin an invisible web across every part of this hall." "Invisible web!" snorted Tiger. He decided to make *himself* invisible instead.

Tiger crept to the back of the hall.
He turned the dial on his watch and ...

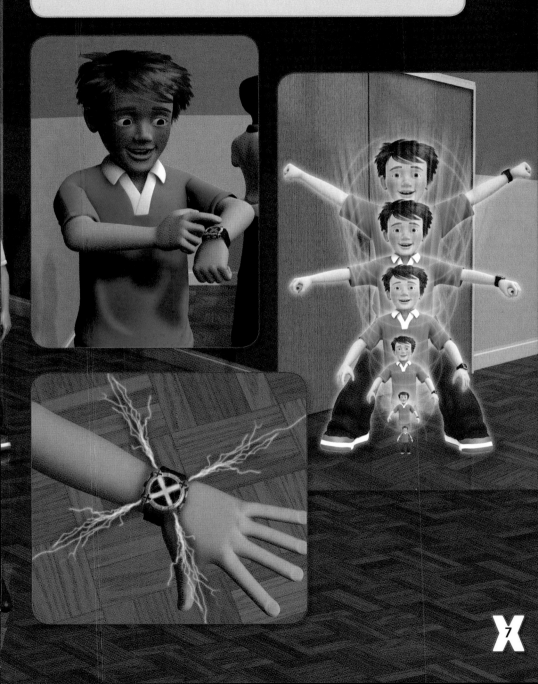

"Where's Tiger?" whispered Max, a few moments later.

"I think I can guess," Cat sighed. "Look!"

She pointed at her watch. A small red dot was flashing on it. It meant that Tiger had shrunk. The dot moved around the watch-face.

"Oh, no!" groaned Max.

Chapter 3 - The Thing ...

The store cupboard was dark and gloomy. Tiger tapped the torch button on his watch and swung it around, full-beam.

Lost Property

Bats and Balls

Tiger's plastic ball was in the lost property box. He grinned and climbed up to fetch it. Tiger pulled himself up on to the edge of the box.

Suddenly, his watch started flashing.

"X-bot alert?" said Tiger, reading the words on the screen. "What does that mean?"

He heard a noise behind him. It sounded like the patter of tiny feet … tiny, spidery feet. Slowly, Tiger turned round. That's when he saw the Thing.

Meanwhile ...

"Well done, everybody!" called Miss Jones. "I've never seen such brilliant spiders. Or such a brilliant web! Now, stay as still as you can. Remember, we're trying to catch a fly!"

"I'd rather catch Tiger," Max muttered.

"He's in the cupboard," whispered Cat.

"Come on," said Max. "Let's get him out before Miss Jones sees that he's gone!"

They started creeping slowly towards the cupboard.

Store Cupboard

Chapter 4 – In the cupboard

The Thing bleeped and stepped forwards. Tiger screamed and stepped back. The lost property box began to rock like a see-saw. The Thing came towards Tiger.

"Help! Help!" he shouted. "It's a, a …"

Tiger did not know what it was but it looked very spidery.

Tiger leapt off the box. He made
a grab for one of the skipping ropes
and swung across the cupboard. The
box fell from the shelf and flipped the
Thing high in the air.

The box and the Thing landed on a net full of footballs. The net burst open. The balls bounced around like a mad penalty shoot-out.

"I don't need this much football practice!" Tiger howled.

Luckily, he spotted his own ball coming towards him. Quickly, he dived like a goalie through one of the holes and hid inside.

The Thing tumbled past Tiger. It was bleeping. It looked just as scared as he was. Tiger stared at it in surprise.

Bleep! Bleep!

Chapter 5 - Good drama

The drama class had never been so quiet.
Everyone was looking at the store cupboard.

"That didn't sound like a fly, Miss,"
someone gasped. "It sounded like a herd
of elephants!"

"It sounded like Tiger to me!" said
Max quietly.

Store Cupboard

Miss Jones walked over to the store cupboard and flung open the door. This was a big mistake. There was a clattering and tumbling as everything spilled out on to the floor.

"Don't worry, Miss!" said Max, quick as a flash. "Cat and I will help you clear it up."

Nobody noticed as Cat picked up Tiger inside his plastic ball. She hurried out of the way, to the other side of the hall. Tiger crawled out of the ball. A moment later, he was normal size again.

As they were clearing up, Miss Jones stepped on something. "Oh dear," she cried out. "I think I've broken one of the toys in the lost property box." She held it out.

It was the Thing. It looked all squashed. It was not bleeping any more.

"Miss Jones," said Max. "Can I try and fix it? I'll get my friend Ant to help."

"Thank you, Max," said Miss Jones, as she handed him the squashed Thing. Then she looked around.

"Look at Tiger everyone!" she exclaimed. "He's still hunched-up like a spider. Now that's what I call good drama!"

Want to find out what happens to the Thing? Then read *Message in an X-bot.*